Contents

Slip Knot 4

Slingshot Cast On 5

Knit Stitch 6

Purl Stitch 7

Binding Off 8

Basic Fabrics 9

Understanding Instructions 12

Additional Techniques 14

Increases 16

Decreases 18

Finishing 20

Dishcloths 22

Scarf 24

Hat 26

Baby Gift Set 28

Mittens 31

Pillow 34

Baby Blanket 36

Dog Coat 38

Textured Stripes Afghan 41

Vest 44

Yarn Information 48

Basic Materials

Knitting really only takes two things – a pair of knitting needles and yarn. There are many sizes of needles – try using a pair of 10" (25.5 cm) straight knitting needles, size 8 (5 mm) for learning. Yarn is available in a multitude of sizes and colors, but for learning we recommend a ball or skein of medium weight yarn in a color you like – but not too dark – a light or bright color will make it easier to see your stitches.

Look for this icon on the yarn label.

Let's Start Knitting!

Slip Knot

Knitting begins with a slip knot. This easy knot will anchor your stitches to the needle and will also count as your first stitch.

Pull a 24" (61 cm) length of yarn from the ball. Make a circle on top of the working yarn (the yarn coming from the ball) *(Fig. 1a)*.

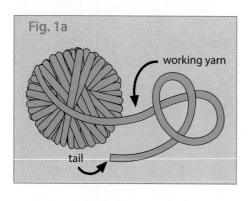

Fig. 1a

working yarn

tail

Insert the needle under the strand in the middle of the circle *(Fig. 1b)*.

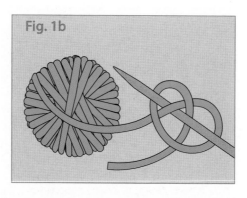

Fig. 1b

Pull on both ends of the yarn to tighten the slip knot *(Fig. 1c)*. To tighten the loop on the needle, pull the tail.

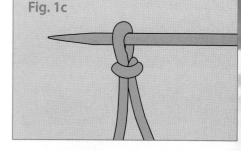

Fig. 1c

The slip knot counts as your first stitch on the needle.

Practice making a slip knot until you feel confident with this simple beginning stitch.

In order to begin knitting, it is necessary to cast on a foundation row of stitches on the needle, see page 5.

Slingshot Cast On

"Cast on" is a term used to describe placing a foundation row of stitches on the needle.

Step 1: Pull a 24" length of yarn from the ball. Make a slip knot *(Figs. 1a-c, page 4)* at the measured distance, pulling gently on the tail to tighten the stitch on the needle (counts as first cast on stitch).

Step 2: Hold the needle in your right hand with your index finger resting on the stitch.

Step 3: Place the tail end over your left thumb and bring the working yarn up and around your index finger. Hold both yarn strands in your palm with your remaining fingers *(Fig. 2a)*.

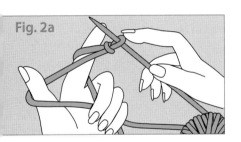

Fig. 2a

Step 4: Insert the needle tip **under** the strand of yarn on your thumb *(Fig. 2b)*.

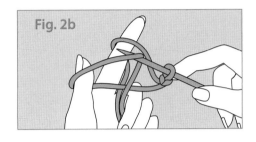

Fig. 2b

Step 5: Bring the needle **over** and around the strand on your index finger *(Fig. 2c)*.

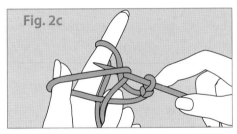

Fig. 2c

Step 6: Pull the yarn and the needle down through the loop on your thumb *(Fig. 2d)*.

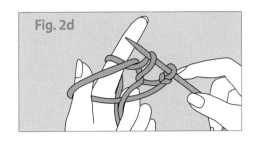

Fig. 2d

Step 7: Drop the loop off your thumb while still holding the yarn strands in your palm. Spread your left thumb and index finger to tighten your new stitch on the needle *(Fig. 2e)*.

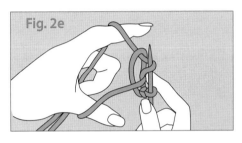

Fig. 2e

Repeat Steps 4-7 for each additional stitch.

After all of your stitches have been cast on, the yarn end may be cut shorter, but leave the end long enough to be woven in later. If the yarn end will be needed to sew a seam, it can be rolled in a ball and pinned to the bottom of the piece after a few rows have been worked.

Continue to cast on stitches until you feel comfortable casting on. With practice, your stitches will become neat and even.

helpful hints

To figure how much yarn is needed for casting on, allow approximately 1" (2.5 cm) of yarn for each stitch to be cast on. Finer yarns require slightly less than 1" (2.5 cm) per stitch, and heavier yarns require slightly more.

Each cast on stitch needs to be snug, but not tight. This will allow you to easily insert the tip of the needle into the stitch when working the first row. The foundation row needs to be as elastic as the knitting.

Knit Stitch

Here is the first of the only two stitches that you need to know for knitting. Follow the steps of Row 1 on this page to learn how easy it is to form the knit stitch. Once you've accomplished this stitch, you are halfway there on your journey to becoming a knitter!

Let's make a practice swatch.
You will knit and purl a total of 16 rows to make the swatch. When you finish, you will have experienced both the knit stitch and the purl stitch.

Cast on 20 stitches.

ROW 1

Step 1: Hold the needle with the cast on stitches in your left hand and the empty needle in your right hand.

Step 2: With the working yarn to the **back** of the needles, slide the right needle into the stitch closest to the tip of the left needle as shown in Fig. 3a.

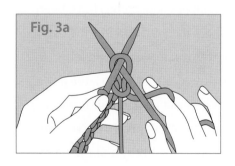
Fig. 3a

Step 3: Hold both needles between your left thumb and fingers. Bring the yarn around the right needle and **between** the needles *(Fig. 3b)* and pull down, tightening the yarn.

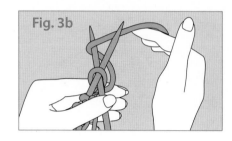
Fig. 3b

Step 4: With your right hand, bring the tip of the right needle under the left needle through the stitch, pulling the loop toward you and through the stitch *(Figs. 3c & d)*.

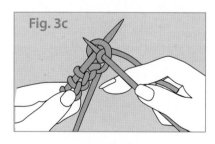
Fig. 3c

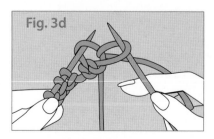
Fig. 3d

Step 5: Slip the old stitch off the left needle and tug on the working yarn to tighten the new stitch *(Fig. 3e)*.

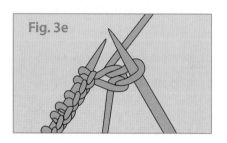
Fig. 3e

Follow Steps 2-5 to knit each stitch across the needle; you should have 20 stitches on your right needle at the end of the row.

ROWS 2-8

To begin the next row, turn your work, placing the needle with the stitches in your left hand and the empty needle in your right hand.

Now that you've learned the knit stitch, you've completed half of your practice swatch. Let's learn the purl stitch next.

You'll find that knitting will become easier and your work will be more even with a little bit of practice.

Purl Stitch

Now you're ready to learn purl, the "other stitch." Knitting becomes easy to understand when you realize that knit stitches and purl stitches are the reverse of each other. In each case, you pull a new stitch through an existing stitch. When knitting, you drop the old stitch off to the back of your work. When purling, the old stitch falls to the front of your work.

helpful hints

When knitting or purling a stitch, wrap the working yarn around the shaft of the needle. Wrapping the yarn around the tip of the needle will make your stitches too tight.

ROW 9

Step 1: Hold the needle with the stitches in your left hand and the empty needle in your right hand.

Step 2: With the yarn in **front** of the needles, slide the tip of the right needle into the stitch closest to the tip of the left needle as shown in Fig. 4a.

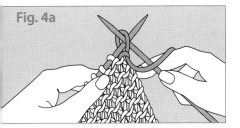
Fig. 4a

Step 3: Hold both needles between your left thumb and fingers while you bring the yarn **between** the needles and around the right needle *(Fig. 4b)* and tighten the yarn.

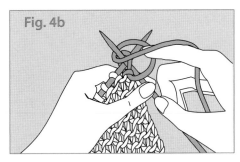
Fig. 4b

Step 4: With your right hand, bring the tip of the right needle through the stitch, pulling the loop away from you and through the stitch *(Fig. 4c)*. Slip the old stitch off the left needle and tug on the working yarn to tighten the new stitch.

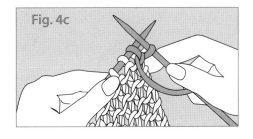
Fig. 4c

Repeat Steps 2-4 across the row.

ROWS 10-16

Turn your work, switching your needles; repeat Steps 2-4 across.

Follow the steps on the next page to bind off all stitches.

Remember, this is only a practice swatch. It doesn't have to be perfect. However, if at any time you're not happy with your work, or if you've made a mistake and would like to correct it, you can. Turn to page 15 to find out how to pick up dropped stitches and how to rip back.

All knitting ends with binding off, locking each stitch as you remove it from the needle. Binding off is also used for shaping and to work buttonholes and pockets.

Let's practice binding off on the swatch you just made.

Step 1: Knit 2 stitches.

Step 2: With the left needle, bring the first stitch over the second stitch and off the needle *(Fig. 5a)*. One stitch has been bound off and one stitch remains on your right needle *(Fig. 5b)*.

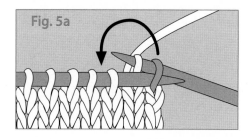
Fig. 5a

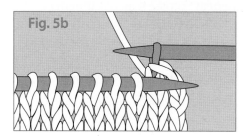
Fig. 5b

Step 3: Knit the next stitch.

Repeat Steps 2 and 3 until only one stitch remains.

Step 4: To lock the last stitch, cut the yarn (leaving a long end) and bring it up through the last stitch *(Fig. 5c)*, pulling to tighten.

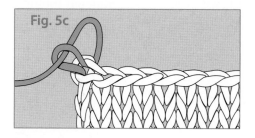
Fig. 5c

Now that you've finished your swatch, you're ready to learn about basic fabrics. We've included instructions for three more swatches on pages 9-11 so you can practice making fabrics.

---

helpful hint

Count stitches as you bind off.
It takes two stitches to bind off one stitch. Count each stitch as you bind it off, not as you knit it.
Bind off loosely versus tightly: Bind off loosely for an edge with elasticity, and bind off tightly for a firm edge. When binding off a crew neck or turtleneck ribbing, always bind off loosely. The bound-off stitches should stretch as much as the ribbing does. To make this easier, replace the needle in your right hand with a larger size needle. To guarantee that the shoulders of a garment will always stay firmly in place and will not sag or droop, bind off tightly. Always bind off tightly when using cotton yarn because of its tendency to stretch.

Basic Fabrics

Using the two basic stitches you've just learned – knit and purl – you can easily make fabrics that occur frequently in knitting.

GARTER STITCH

Knitting every stitch in every row, as you did in the first 8 rows of your swatch, is called Garter Stitch *(Photo A)*. Look closely at your swatch and you will see that each stitch looks like the **green** stitch in Fig. 6.

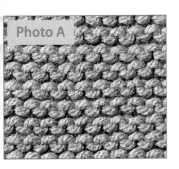

Photo A

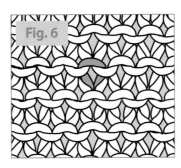

Fig. 6

Two rows of knitting make one horizontal ridge in your fabric. Garter Stitch is a thick, reversible fabric that does not curl at the edges. You can also achieve Garter Stitch by **purling** every stitch in every row, as you did on Rows 9-16 of your swatch.

Take a look!

We've created bonus videos for you @ www.leisurearts.com/6395

STOCKINETTE STITCH

Stockinette Stitch is the most common knit fabric and is the result of alternating knit and purl rows.

Let's make another swatch while you learn how to knit Stockinette Stitch.

Cast on 20 stitches.

Row 1: Knit each stitch across the row *(page 6)*.

Row 2: Purl each stitch across the row *(page 7)*.

Rows 3-8: Repeat Rows 1 and 2, 3 times.

Bind off your stitches *(page 8)*.

Look at the **knit** side of your fabric *(Photo B)*. This is considered to be the right side of your work. Notice that your fabric is smooth and flat, and that the side edges curl under. Each stitch should resemble a "V" like the **green** stitch in Fig. 7.

Photo B

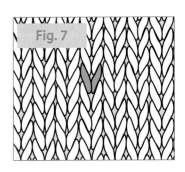

Fig. 7

Reverse Stockinette Stitch

Reverse Stockinette Stitch is worked the same as Stockinette Stitch with the exception that the **purl** side of your fabric is considered to be the right side.

Now flip your Stockinette Stitch swatch over and look at the purl side of your fabric (*Photo C*). The fabric is bumpy, and the side edges curl slightly toward you.

Photo C

Each stitch should resemble a bump like the **green** stitch in Fig. 8.

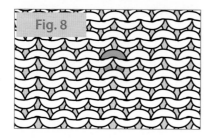

Fig. 8

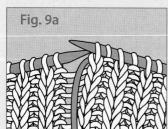
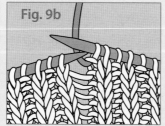
Seed (or Moss) Stitch

Seed Stitch, also known as Moss Stitch, is a reversible fabric that does not curl at the edges (*Photo D*). Alternate the knit and purl stitches on the first row. On the following rows, knit the purl stitches and purl the knit stitches as they face you (*Fig. 10*).

Let's work a swatch as you learn to knit Seed (or Moss) Stitch.

Photo D

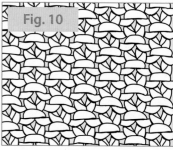

Fig. 10

Note: These instructions are for an even number of stitches.

Cast on 20 stitches (*abbreviated sts*).

Row 1: ★ K1, P1; repeat from ★ across.

Translation: Knit the first stitch (*abbreviated K1*), purl the next stitch (*abbreviated P1*), ★ K1, P1; repeat from ★ (all the instructions between the first ★ and the semicolon) across the row.

Note: See Understanding Instructions (*page 12*).

Row 2: ★ P1, K1; repeat from ★ across.

Row 3: ★ K1, P1; repeat from ★ across.

Rows 4-9: Repeat Rows 2 and 3, 3 times for Seed (or Moss) Stitch.

Bind off all sts in pattern.

Ribbing

Ribbing is a wonderful elastic stitch that's often worked at the bottom of sweaters, on cuffs, and around necklines. It can be worked in several combinations of knit and purl stitches, the most common one being "knit one, purl one" ribbing, which offers more stretch than other ribbing variations.

Alternate the knit and purl stitches on the first row. On the following rows, knit the knit stitches and purl the purl stitches as they face you.

The most common ribbing is knit 1, purl 1 ribbing *(abbreviated K1, P1 ribbing) (Fig. 11a).*

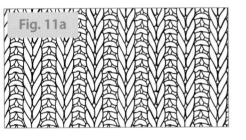
Fig. 11a

Knit 2, purl 2 ribbing *(abbreviated K2, P2 ribbing)* is not quite as elastic as K1, P1 ribbing and is worked in the same manner over a multiple of 4 stitches *(Fig. 11b).*

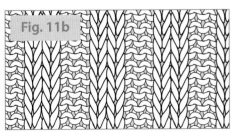
Fig. 11b

Let's make another swatch while you learn to knit Ribbing.

Note: These instructions are for an even number of stitches.

Cast on 20 sts **loosely**.

Row 1: ★ K1, P1; repeat from ★ across.

Rows 2-8: Repeat Row 1, 7 times for K1, P1 ribbing.

Bind off all sts in pattern.

Compare your ribbing to Photo E. Notice that the vertical lines of "V's" (the knit stitches) almost hide the bumps (the purl stitches). When working ribbing, the "V's" must always be knit and the bumps must always be purled *(Figs. 11a & b).*

Photo E

If you would like to take a break from learning new things, knit a useful kitchen dishcloth on page 22.

helpful hint

Bind off in pattern. Unless otherwise stated, when you're instructed to bind off your stitches, you should always bind off in pattern. In reality, you're working another row.

If you would knit the next row, knit the stitches as you're binding them off. If you would purl the next row, purl the stitches as you're binding them off. If you're doing both, knit and purl the stitches as you're binding them off, as you would if it was a normal row. Binding off ribbing in pattern maintains the elasticity of the ribbing.

Whether you're binding off at the shoulders, the back of the neck, or around the neck or armhole ribbing, your work will be more professional in appearance if that row is worked in pattern.

Understanding Instructions

Knit instructions are written using abbreviations, symbols, terms, and punctuation marks. This method of writing saves time and space, and is actually easy to read once you understand the knit shorthand.

Abbreviations

A list of abbreviations will be included with each book, and you should review this list carefully before beginning a project. The list below gives those used for the projects in this book.

cm	centimeters
K	knit
M1	make one
mm	millimeters
P	purl
PSSO	pass slipped stitch over
SSK	slip, slip, knit
SSP	slip, slip, purl
st(s)	stitch(es)
tbl	through back loop(s)
tog	together
YO	yarn over

Symbols & Terms

★ — work all instructions following a ★ (star) as many **more** times as indicated in addition to the first time.

change to larger size needles — replace the right needle with one larger size needle and work the stitches from the left needle as instructed; at the end of the row, replace the left needle with the other larger size needle.

loosely — (binding off, adding new, or casting on stitches) the work should be as elastic as the knitting.

right vs. left — the side of the garment as if you were wearing it.

right side vs. wrong side — the right side of your work is the side that will show when the piece is finished.

work even — work without increasing or decreasing in the established pattern.

◼◻◻◻ **BEGINNER**	Projects for first-time knitters using basic knit and purl stitches. Minimal shaping.
◼◼◻◻ **EASY**	Projects using basic stitches, repetitive stitch patterns, simple color changes, and simple shaping and finishing.
◼◼◼◻ **INTERMEDIATE**	Projects with a variety of stitches, such as basic cables and lace, simple intarsia, double-pointed needles and knitting in the round needle techniques, mid-level shaping and finishing.
◼◼◼◼ **EXPERIENCED**	Projects using advanced techniques and stitches, such as short rows, fair isle, more intricate intarsia, cables, lace patterns, and numerous color changes.

Punctuation

When reading knitting instructions, read from punctuation mark to punctuation mark. Just as in reading, a period indicates a stop and commas (,) and semicolons (;) indicate a pause.

colon (:) — the number(s) given after a colon at the end of a row or round denote(s) the number of stitches you should have on that row or round. When repeating rows, the number given is for the last row.

braces { } — contain information or instructions pertaining to multiple sizes.

parentheses ( ) or brackets [ ] — indicate repetition, so you should work the enclosed instructions **as many** times as specified by the number immediately following. Parentheses or brackets may also contain explanatory remarks.

Terminology

U.S. and International terminologies differ slightly. Equivalents are:

KNIT TERMINOLOGY	
UNITED STATES	**INTERNATIONAL**
gauge =	tension
bind off =	cast off
yarn over (YO) =	yarn forward (yfwd) **or** yarn around needle (yrn)

Gauge

Gauge is the number of stitches and rows per inch and is used to determine the finished size of a project. Most knitting patterns specify the gauge that you must match to ensure proper size or fit and to ensure you have enough yarn to complete the project. Before beginning any knitted item, it is absolutely necessary for you to knit a sample swatch in the pattern stitch with the weight of yarn and needle size suggested. It must be large enough for you to measure your gauge, usually a 4" (10 cm) square. After completing the swatch, measure it. If your swatch is larger or smaller than specified, make another, changing needle size (see chart at bottom of page) to get the correct gauge. Remember, DO NOT HESITATE TO CHANGE THE NEEDLE SIZE IN ORDER TO OBTAIN CORRECT GAUGE. Once you have obtained the correct gauge, you should continue to measure the total width of your work frequently to be sure your gauge does not change.

Yarn Weight Symbol & Names	LACE 0	SUPER FINE 1	FINE 2	LIGHT 3	MEDIUM 4	BULKY 5	SUPER BULKY 6
Type of Yarns in Category	Fingering, size 10 crochet thread	Sock, Fingering, Baby	Sport, Baby	DK, Light Worsted	Worsted, Afghan, Aran	Chunky, Craft, Rug	Bulky, Roving
Knit Gauge Range* in Stockinette St to 4" (10 cm)	33-40** sts	27-32 sts	23-26 sts	21-24 sts	16-20 sts	12-15 sts	6-11 sts
Advised Needle Size Range	000-1	1 to 3	3 to 5	5 to 7	7 to 9	9 to 11	11 and larger

*GUIDELINES ONLY: The chart above reflects the most commonly used gauges and needle sizes for specific yarn categories.

** Lace weight yarns are usually knitted on larger needles to create lacy openwork patterns. Accordingly, a gauge range is difficult to determine. Always follow the gauge stated in your pattern.

KNITTING NEEDLES																			
U.S.	0	1	2	3	4	5	6	7	8	9	10	10½	11	13	15	17	19	35	50
U.K.	13	12	11	10	9	8	7	6	5	4	3	2	1	00	000	---	---	---	---
Metric - mm	2	2.25	2.75	3.25	3.5	3.75	4	4.5	5	5.5	6	6.5	8	9	10	12.75	15	19	25

Additional Techniques

Here are a variety of techniques you'll encounter as you knit. You can take the time to learn about all of them now or refer to each as needed.

Front and Back Loops

Always work into the front of a stitch unless instructed to work through back loop *(abbreviated tbl) (Fig. 12)*.

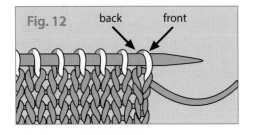

Fig. 12   back   front

Twisted Stitches

When instructed to knit or purl through the **back** loop of a stitch *(Fig. 12)*, the result will be twisted stitches *(Fig. 13)*.

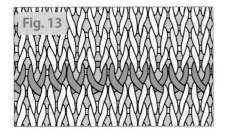

Fig. 13

Sometimes twisted stitches are used for a special effect.

Slipping Stitches

A slipped stitch is a stitch transferred from the left needle to the right needle, without knitting or purling it.

When slipping stitches, in order to prevent twisted stitches, the general rule is, when you're not going to use the slipped stitch again until the next row, slip it as if to **purl** *(Fig. 14a)*, keeping the front loop to the front. When you're going to use the slipped stitch again on the same row, as in a decrease, slip it as if to **knit** *(Fig. 14b)*. This will only temporarily twist the stitch.

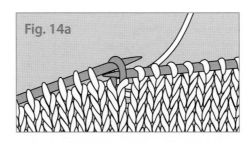

Fig. 14a

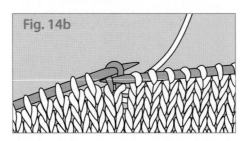

Fig. 14b

Join New Yarn

Always join new yarn at the beginning of a row, so the ends can be woven in a seam and not be visible on the finished project. Cut the existing yarn leaving a 6" (15 cm) end. Begin the next row with the new ball of yarn, leaving a 6" (15 cm) end to weave in later *(see Weaving in Yarn Ends, page 21)*.

Markers

As a convenience to you, we've used markers to help distinguish the beginning of a pattern or the beginning of a round. You may use purchased markers that fit on your needle or you may tie a length of contrasting color yarn around the needle.

Place markers as instructed. When you reach a marker on a row, slip it from the left needle to the right needle *(Fig. 15)*; remove it when no longer needed.

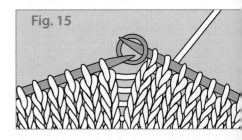

Fig. 15

Dropped Stitches

A dropped stitch is a stitch that accidentally slips off your needle and may easily unravel more than one row. It can happen to anyone, but there's an easy solution that will save the day.

To pick up a dropped stitch, hold the work with the **knit** side facing, insert a crochet hook through the loop of the dropped stitch, hook the strand of yarn immediately above it *(Fig. 16a)*, and pull it through the loop on your hook. Continue in this manner until you have used all of the strands of yarn.

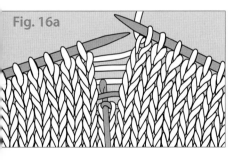

Fig. 16a

If you were knitting across the row, slip the stitch onto the left needle with the right side of the stitch to the front *(Fig. 16b)*.

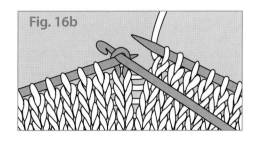

Fig. 16b

If you were purling across the row, slip the stitch onto the right needle with the right side of the stitch to the front. Turn your work again to finish the row.

If a mistake is on the row you just worked, turn the work around so that you are holding the needle with the mistake in your left hand, ★ insert the **right** needle from the **back** into the stitch **below** the next stitch on the left needle *(Fig. 16c)*, slip the stitch off the **left** needle and gently pull the working yarn to unravel the old stitch; repeat from ★ across until the mistake has been eliminated. Turn your work again to finish the row.

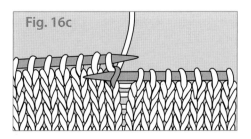

Fig. 16c

If you discover a mistake in a previous row or if you have not maintained correct gauge, it will be necessary to rip out more than one row. Place a safety pin or paper clip through the first and the last stitch in the row with the mistake. Slide all the stitches off the needles and rip back to the first safety pin or paper clip. Hold your knitting in your left hand with the working yarn at the right. ★ Insert a needle from the **back** into the stitch **below** the first stitch and gently pull the working yarn to unravel the old stitch; repeat from ★ until all the stitches are back on a needle.

> **helpful hint**
>
> There will be much less chance of dropping or splitting stitches if the stitches are picked up with a needle 2 or 3 sizes smaller than the one used to knit them.

Increases

The knit increase is the most common increase used. It uses one stitch to make two stitches. The make one increase and yarn overs do not use a stitch to make more stitches.

Increase Evenly Across

When increasing across the row, the important point is to reach the total number of stitches needed with the increases spaced as evenly as possible.

Add one to the number of increases required and divide that number into the number of stitches on the needle. Subtract one from the result and the new number is the appropriate number of stitches to be worked between each increase. Adjust the number as needed. Sometimes it's necessary to work more or fewer stitches between increases to arrive at the correct total number of stitches.

Knit Increase

To make a knit increase, knit the next stitch but do **not** slip the old stitch off the left needle *(Fig. 17a)*. Insert the right needle into the **back** loop of the **same** stitch *(Fig. 17b)* and knit it, then slip the old stitch off the left needle.

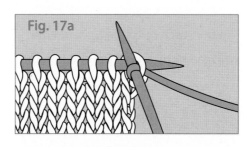

Fig. 17a

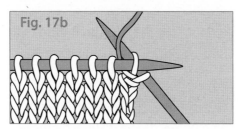

Fig. 17b

Make One Increase

The make one increase forms a new stitch by working into the strand between two stitches. The strand is intentionally twisted in order to prevent a hole.

To Make One *(abbreviated M1)*, insert the **left** needle under the horizontal strand between the stitches from the **front** *(Fig. 18a)*. Then knit into the **back** of the strand *(Fig. 18b)*, slipping it off the left needle.

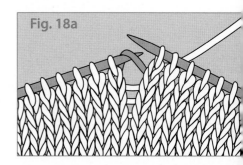

Fig. 18a

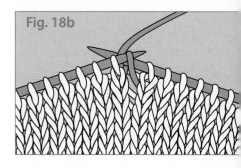

Fig. 18b

Yarn Overs

A yarn over (abbreviated YO), another type of increase, is simply placing the yarn over the right needle, creating an extra stitch.

Since the yarn over does produce a hole in the fabric, it's used for a lacy effect or a buttonhole. On the row following a yarn over, you must be careful to keep it on the needle and treat it as a stitch by knitting or purling it as instructed.

After a knit stitch, before a knit stitch: Bring the yarn forward **between** the needles, then back **over** the top of the right needle, so that it is now in position to knit the next stitch *(Fig. 19a)*.

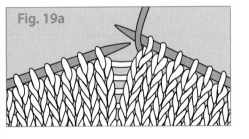
Fig. 19a

After a purl stitch, before a purl stitch: Take the yarn **over** the right needle to the back, then forward **under** it, so that it is now in position to purl the next stitch *(Fig. 19b)*.

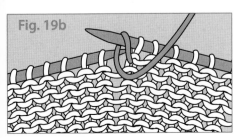
Fig. 19b

After a knit stitch, before a purl stitch: Take the yarn forward **between** the needles, then back **over** the top of the right needle and forward **between** the needles again, so that it is now in position to purl the next stitch *(Fig. 19c)*.

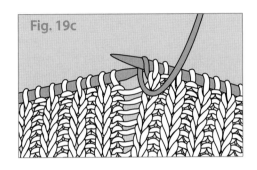
Fig. 19c

After a purl stitch, before a knit stitch: Take the yarn **over** the right needle to the back, so that it is now in position to knit the next stitch *(Fig. 19d)*.

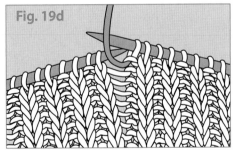
Fig. 19d

Adding New Stitches

Adding new stitches is a technique used when you need to add on more than one stitch at the beginning or in the middle of a row, such as for the thumb of the mittens or the armhole band on the vest.

Knit the next stitch, but do **not** slip the old stitch off the left needle *(Fig. 20a)*, insert the left needle into the loop just worked from **front** to **back** and slip it onto the left needle *(Fig. 20b)*. Repeat for the required number of stitches.

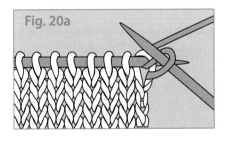
Fig. 20a

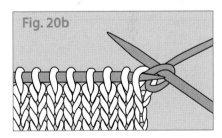
Fig. 20b

Decreases

A decrease is made when two or more stitches are worked together to form one stitch.

Decreases can be worked on either the right or wrong side of your fabric. They are used to form decorative patterns and also for armhole and neck shaping.

A decrease will slant either to the right or to the left. Decreases worked at the edge of a piece for shaping usually lean in the same direction as the knitting is shaped. We have indicated which direction each decrease will slant.

Knit 2 Together

To Knit 2 Together *(abbreviated K2 tog)*, insert the right needle into the **front** of the first two stitches on the left needle as if to **knit** *(Fig. 21)*, then **knit** them together as if they were one stitch. (This decrease slants to the **right**.)

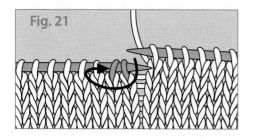

Fig. 21

The knit two together decrease is the most common knit decrease.

Knit 3 Together

To Knit 3 Together *(abbreviated K3 tog)*, insert the right needle into the **front** of the first three stitches on the left needle as if to **knit** *(Fig. 22)*, then **knit** them together as if they were one stitch. (This decrease slants to the **right**.)

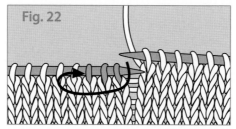

Fig. 22

Slip, Slip, Knit

To Slip, Slip, Knit *(abbreviated SSK)*, with the yarn in back of the work, separately slip two stitches as if to **knit** *(Fig. 23a)*. Insert the **left** needle into the **front** of both slipped sts *(Fig. 23b)* and **knit** them together as if they were one stitch *(Fig. 23c)*. (This decrease slants to the **left**.)

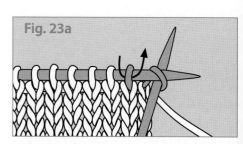

Fig. 23a

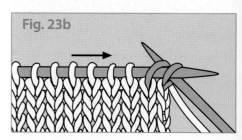

Fig. 23b

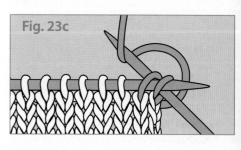

Fig. 23c

Take a look!

Remember you can see videos of all these stitches @ www.leisurearts.com/6395

Slip 1, Knit 1, Pass Slipped Stitch Over

To Slip 1, Knit 1, Pass Slipped Stitch Over *(abbreviated slip 1, K1, PSSO)*, slip one stitch as if to **knit** *(Fig. 14b, page 14)*, then knit the next stitch. With the left needle, bring the slipped stitch over the knit stitch *(Fig. 24)* and off the needle. (This decrease slants to the **left**.)

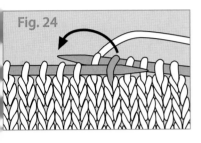

Fig. 24

The slip one, knit one, PSSO decrease and the slip, slip, knit decrease are interchangeable.

The purl two together decrease is the most common purl decrease.

Slip 1, Knit 2 Together, Pass Slipped Stitch Over

To Slip 1, Knit 2 Together, Pass Slipped Stitch Over *(abbreviated slip 1, K2 tog, PSSO)*, slip one stitch as if to **knit** *(Fig. 14b, page 14)*, then knit the next two stitches together *(Fig. 21, page 18)*. With the left needle, bring the slipped stitch over the stitch just made *(Fig. 25)* and off the needle. (This decrease slants to the **left**.)

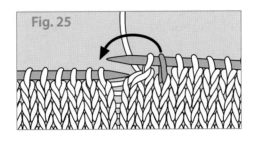

Fig. 25

The slip one, knit two together, PSSO decrease uses three stitches and decreases two stitches. It's frequently used in lace patterns like the Baby Blanket.

Purl 2 Together

To Purl 2 Together *(abbreviated P2 tog)*, insert the right needle into the **front** of the first two stitches on the left needle as if to **purl** *(Fig. 26)*, then **purl** them together as if they were one stitch. (This decrease slants to the **right** on the knit side.)

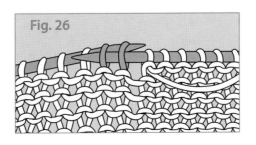

Fig. 26

Purl 2 Together Through Back Loop

To Purl 2 Together Through Back Loop *(abbreviated P2 tog tbl)*, insert the right needle into the **back** loop of the next two stitches from **back** to **front** *(Fig. 27)*, then **purl** them together as if they were one stitch. (This decrease slants to the **left** on the knit side.)

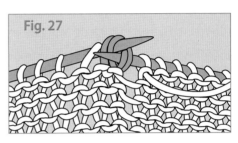

Fig. 27

Slip, Slip, Purl

To Slip, Slip, Purl *(abbreviated SSP)*, with yarn held in front of work, separately slip two stitches as if to **knit** *(Fig. 23a, page 18)*. Place these two stitches back onto the left needle. Insert the right needle into the **back** loop of both stitches from **back** to **front** *(Fig. 28)* and purl them together as if they were one stitch. (This decrease slants to the **left** on the knit side.)

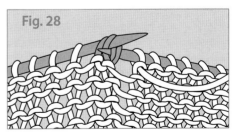

Fig. 28

The slip, slip, purl decrease resembles the slip, slip, knit decrease.

The assembly and finishing of a design should be done with great care. The techniques given will add value and beauty to your finished projects.

Picking Up Stitches

Some projects require you to pick up stitches. Picking up stitches along the edge of a piece allows you to add a band on the dog coat. Stitches can also be picked up in the middle of a row as in the mittens.

When instructed to pick up stitches, insert the needle from the **front** to the **back** under two strands at the edge of the worked piece *(Figs. 29a & b)*. Wrap the yarn around the needle as if to **knit**, then bring the needle with the yarn back through the stitch to the right side, resulting in a stitch on the needle.

Repeat this along the edge, picking up the required number of stitches.

A crochet hook may be helpful to pull yarn through.

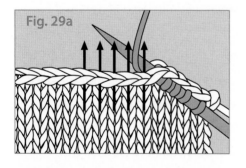
Fig. 29a

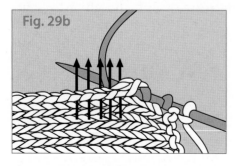
Fig. 29b

Weaving Seams

A tapestry or yarn needle is best to use for sewing (or weaving) seams because the blunt tip will not split the yarn. Use the same yarn your project was made with to sew the seams. However, if the yarn is textured or bulky, it may be easier to sew the seam with a small, smooth yarn of the same color, such as tapestry yarn or an acrylic needlepoint yarn. Seam weaving is practically invisible and does not add bulk.

With the **right** side of both pieces facing you and the edges even, sew through both sides once to secure the seam. Insert the needle under the bar **between** the first and second stitches on the row and pull the yarn through *(Fig. 30)*. Insert the needle under the next bar on the second side. Repeat from side to side, being careful to match rows. If the edges are different lengths, it may be necessary to insert the needle under two bars at one edge.

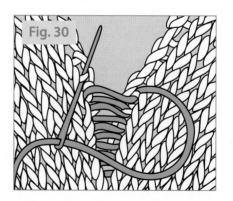
Fig. 30

helpful hint

If a different yarn is used for the seams, be sure the care instructions for both yarns are the same. If the yarn used to knit your project is machine washable, the seam yarn must also be machine washable.

Twisted Cord

The twisted cord is easy to make and can be used as a tie for booties and hats.

Cut 2 pieces of yarn, each 3 times as long as the desired finished length **or** to the length specified in the instructions. Holding both pieces of yarn together, fasten one end to a stationary object or have another person hold it; twist until **tight**. Fold in half and let it twist itself; knot both ends and cut the loops on the folded end.

Weaving in Yarn Ends

Thread a yarn needle with the yarn end. With **wrong** side facing, weave the needle through a seam or through a few inches of stitches following the contour of the stitches, then reverse the direction and weave it back through several more inches. When the end is secure, clip the yarn off close to your work.

Pom-Pom

Pom-poms are great to add to the top of a hat, like the one included in the Baby Gift Set, and to lots of other projects.

Cut a piece of cardboard 3" (7.5 cm) square. Wind the yarn around the cardboard lengthwise until it is approximately ½" (12 mm) thick in the middle *(Fig. 31a)*. Carefully slip the yarn off the cardboard and firmly tie an 18" (45.5 cm) length of yarn around the middle *(Fig. 31b)*. Leave yarn ends long enough to attach the pom-pom. Cut the loops on both ends, shake the pom-pom to fluff the strands, and trim the pom-pom into a smooth ball *(Fig. 31c)*.

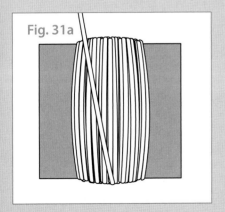
Fig. 31a

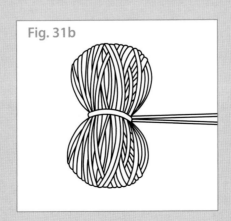
Fig. 31b

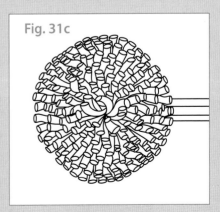
Fig. 31c

Take a look at the 12 great projects we've selected especially for the beginning knitter. We've listed the projects in order of degree of difficulty, with the simplest first. When you're comfortable making the knit and purl stitches, and the basic knit fabrics, you're ready to begin a project! The extra skills needed to complete each project are specified in the instructions and can be learned as you go.

Choose your favorite projects and get ready to have fun!

Blue Dishcloth

The Blue Dishcloth uses knit and purl stitches to create an attractive textured design. The Variegated Dishcloth is made in the same manner as the seed stitch swatch you made on page 10, except that you use an odd number of stitches. Soon you'll be able to finish a couple of rows in 10 minutes! These are perfect beginner projects and can be taken with you wherever you go, since they require only a small amount of cotton yarn to make each one. Let's knit!

◼◼☐☐☐ **BEGINNER**

Finished Size: Approximately 10" (25.5 cm) square

SHOPPING LIST

Yarn (Medium Weight Cotton)
☐ 95 yards (87 meters)

Knitting Needles
Straight needles,
☐ Size 8 (5 mm)

Additional Supplies
☐ Yarn needle

If you come to an abbreviation, symbol, term, or punctuation that you haven't learned yet, refer to Understanding Instructions, page 12.

INSTRUCTIONS

Cast on 46 sts.

Rows 1-4: Knit across.

Row 5 (Right side): K9, P2, (K6, P2) 4 times, K3.

Row 6: K3, P1, K2, (P6, K2) 4 times, P5, K3.

Row 7: K7, P2, (K6, P2) 4 times, K5.

Row 8: K3, P3, K2, (P6, K2) 4 times, P3, K3.

Row 9: K5, P2, (K6, P2) 4 times, K7.

Row 10: K3, P5, K2, (P6, K2) 4 times, P1, K3.

Row 11: K3, purl across to last 3 sts, K3.

Rows 12-16: Repeat Rows 6-10.

Row 17: K3, P2, (K6, P2) 4 times, K9.

Row 18: Knit across.

Rows 19-73: Repeat Rows 5-18, 3 times; then repeat Rows 5-17 once **more**.

Rows 74-77: Knit across.

Bind off all sts in **knit** (page 8).

Weave in yarn ends (page 21).

Design by Linda A. Daley.

Variegated Dishcloth

 ■□□□ **BEGINNER**

Finished Size: Approximately 10" (25.5 cm) square

SHOPPING LIST

Yarn (Medium Weight Cotton) 🧶 MEDIUM 4

☐ 125 yards (114 meters)

Knitting Needles

Straight needles,

☐ Size 7 (4.5 mm)

Additional Supplies

☐ Yarn needle

If you come to an abbreviation, symbol, term, or punctuation that you haven't learned yet, refer to Understanding Instructions, page 12.

INSTRUCTIONS

Cast on 51 sts.

Row 1: K1, ★ P1, K1; repeat from ★ across.

Repeat Row 1 for Seed Stitch until Dishcloth measures approximately 10" (25.5 cm) from cast on edge.

Bind off all sts in pattern *(page 11)*.

Weave in yarn ends *(page 21)*.

Design by Eunice Svinicki.

Scarf

This warm scarf and hat set is made in ribbing like the swatch you made on page 11, except that you use an odd number of stitches for the Scarf. A smaller size needle is used on the first row of each stripe to maintain gauge. The Fashionable Hat design (shown on page 27) also incorporates decreases for shaping. In only 30 minutes, you can see the stripes beginning to form.

 **BEGINNER**

SHOPPING LIST

Yarn (Medium Weight)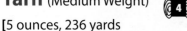

[5 ounces, 236 yards
(141 grams, 215 meters) per skein]:
☐ Grey - 1{2-2} skein(s)
[7 ounces, 364 yards
(198 grams, 33 meters) per skein]:
☐ Burgundy - 30 yards
(27.5 meters)
☐ Lt Grey - small amount

Knitting Needles

Straight needles,
☐ Size 5 (3.75 mm) **and**
☐ Size 6 (4 mm)
or sizes needed for gauge

Additional Supplies

☐ Yarn needle

SIZE INFORMATION

Size: Small {Medium-Large}
Finished Width: 5{7-9}"/12.5{18-23} cm
Finished Length: 36{44-54}"/
91.5{112-137} cm

Size Note: We have printed the sizes in colors to make it easier for you to find:
- Size Small in Blue
- Size Medium in Pink
- Size Large in Green

Instructions in Black apply to all sizes.

GAUGE INFORMATION

See Gauge (page 13).
With larger size needles, in ribbing,
24 sts and 18 rows = 4" (10 cm)

If you come to an abbreviation, symbol, term, or punctuation that you haven't learned yet, refer to Understanding Instructions, page 12.

To Change Colors, pick up the new color leaving an end long enough to weave in later and continue knitting. You may temporarily tie the new color to the old color; just be sure to untie the knot before weaving in the ends.

INSTRUCTIONS
First End

With Grey and larger size needles, cast on 29{41-53} sts.

Row 1: P1, (K1, P1) across.

Row 2 (Right side)**:** K1, (P1, K1) across.

Repeat Rows 1 and 2 for ribbing until Scarf measures approximately 2" (2.5 cm) from cast on edge, ending by working Row 1; cut Grey.

FIRST STRIPE

Row 1: With Burgundy and smaller size needle, knit across.

Row 2: With larger size needle, P1, (K1, P1) across.

Row 3: With larger size needle, K1, (P1, K1) across.

Row 4: With larger size needle, P1, (K1, P1) across; drop Burgundy.

Row 5: With Lt Grey and smaller size needle, knit across.

Hat

Row 6: With larger size needle, P1, (K1, P1) across; cut Lt Grey.

Rows 7-10: Repeat Rows 1-4.

Cut Burgundy.

BODY

Row 1: With Grey and smaller size needle, knit across.

Row 2: With larger size needle, P1, (K1, P1) across.

Row 3: With larger size needle, K1, (P1, K1) across.

Repeat Rows 2 and 3 until Scarf measures approximately 32{40-50}"/81.5{101.5-127} cm from cast on edge, ending by working Row 2.

Second Stripe

Work same as First Stripe.

Second End

Work same as Body for 2" (5 cm).

Bind off all sts in ribbing *(page 11)*.

Weave in yarn ends *(page 21)*.

SHOPPING LIST

Yarn (Medium Weight)

[5 ounces, 236 yards (141 grams, 215 meters) per skein]:

☐ Grey - 1 skein

[7 ounces, 364 yards (198 grams, 33 meters) per skein]:

☐ Burgundy - 15 yards (13.5 meters)

☐ Lt Grey - small amount

Knitting Needles

Straight needles,

☐ Size 5 (3.75 mm) **and**

☐ Size 6 (4 mm)

or sizes needed for gauge

Additional Supplies

☐ Yarn needle

SIZE INFORMATION

Size: Small {Medium-Large}

Finished Circumference:

16{17-18½}"/40.5{43-47} cm

Size Note: We have printed the sizes in colors to make it easier for you to find:

• Size Small in Blue
• Size Medium in Pink
• Size Large in Green

Instructions in Black apply to all sizes.

GAUGE INFORMATION

See Gauge (page 13).

With larger size needles, in ribbing, 24 sts and 18 rows = 4" (10 cm)

TECHNIQUES USED

🎥 K2 tog (**Knit 2 together,** *Fig. 21, page 18*)

🎥 K3 tog (**Knit 3 together,** *Fig. 22, page 18*)

🎥 P2 tog (**Purl 2 together,** *Fig. 26, page 19*)

If you come to an abbreviation, symbol, term, or punctuation that you haven't learned yet, refer to Understanding Instructions, page 12.

See To Change Colors, page 24.

INSTRUCTIONS
Body

With Grey and larger size needles, cast on 96{104-112} sts.

Rows 1-5: (K1, P1) across.

Row 6 (Right side)**:** With Burgundy and smaller size needle, knit across.

Row 7: With larger size needle, (K1, P1) across; drop Burgundy.

Row 8: With Lt Grey and smaller size needle, knit across.

Row 9: With larger size needle, (K1, P1) across; cut Lt Grey.

Row 10: With Burgundy and smaller size needle, knit across.

Row 11: With larger size needle, (K1, P1) across; cut Burgundy.

Row 12: With Grey and smaller size needle, knit across.

Row 13: With larger size needle, (K1, P1) across.

Repeat Row 13 until Hat measures approximately 8{9-10}"/20.5{23-25.5} cm from cast on edge, ending by working a **right** side row.

Shaping

Row 1 (Decrease row)**:** K1, P1, (K3 tog, P1) across to last 2 sts, K1, P1: 50{54-58} sts.

Rows 2-6: (K1, P1) across.

Row 7 (Decrease row)**:** K1, K2 tog across to last st, P1: 26{28-30} sts.

Row 8 (Decrease row)**:** P2 tog across: 13{14-15} sts.

Cut yarn leaving a long end.

Thread a yarn needle with the end and separately slip each stitch from the knitting needle onto the yarn; gather the stitches **tightly** to close, then secure end.

Weave seam *(Fig. 30, page 20)*, remembering that **right** side of brim is **wrong** side of Hat.

Weave in yarn ends *(page 21)*.

Fold bottom edge to form brim.

Baby Gift Set

This cute gift set is made using a combination of Stockinette Stitch and Garter Stitch for a ridged effect. Half of the Bootie can be made in just 30 minutes. Your friends will be so impressed by your new skills at the next baby shower!

■□□□ BEGINNER +

SHOPPING LIST

Yarn (Medium Weight)

[4 ounces, 204 yards
(113 grams, 187 meters) per skein]:
☐ Variegated - 1 skein
[5 ounces, 256 yards
(141 grams, 234 meters) per skein]:
☐ Green - 1 skein

Knitting Needles

Straight needles,
☐ Size 7 (4.5 mm)
or size needed for gauge

Additional Supplies

☐ Yarn needle

GAUGE INFORMATION

See Gauge (page 13).
In Stockinette Stitch (knit one row,
   purl one row),
   20 sts and 28 rows = 4" (10 cm)

Finished Size: 6 months

TECHNIQUES USED

- YO (**Yarn overs,**
  Fig. 19a, page 17)
- K2 tog (**Knit 2 together,**
  Fig. 21, page 18)
- P2 tog (**Purl 2 together,**
  Fig. 26, page 19)

If you come to an abbreviation, symbol, term, or punctuation that you haven't learned yet, refer to Understanding Instructions, page 12.

See To Change Colors, page 24.

INSTRUCTIONS
Cap

With Green, cast on 80 sts.

Rows 1-7: Knit across.

Cut Green; with Variegated and beginning with a **knit** row, work in Stockinette Stitch until piece measures approximately 3½" (9 cm) from cast on edge, ending by working a **purl** row.

SHAPING

Row 1: (K3, K2 tog) across: 64 sts.

Row 2 AND ALL WRONG SIDE ROWS: Purl across.

Row 3: (K2, K2 tog) across: 48 sts.

Row 5: (K1, K2 tog) across: 32 sts.

Row 7: K2 tog across: 16 sts.

Row 9: K2 tog across: 8 sts.

Cut yarn leaving a long end.

Thread a yarn needle with the end and separately slip each stitch from the knitting needle onto the yarn; gather the stitches **tightly** to close, then secure end.

Weave seam (*Fig. 30, page 20*).

EAR FLAP (Make 2)

With Green, cast on 26 sts.

Rows 1 and 2 (Border)**:** Knit across.

🎥 A short row is a row that's not worked all the way from one end to the other. The body of the Ear Flap is worked in Stockinette Stitch, beginning in the center of the Garter Stitch border. Each row works across the center 9 stitches of the body, then a decrease is made using the last stitch on the body and the next stitch on the border. Leaving the remaining stitches unworked, you will stop, **turn** the work, and continue in the opposite direction. **Begin working in short rows as follows:**

Row 3: Cut Green, slip 8 sts as if to **purl** onto right needle; with Variegated P9, P2 tog, leave remaining sts unworked.

Row 4 (Right side)**: Turn;** K9, K2 tog, leave remaining sts unworked.

Row 5: Turn; P9, P2 tog, leave remaining sts unworked.

Rows 6-16: Repeat Rows 4 and 5, 5 times; then repeat Row 4 once **more.**

Slip remaining st on left needle onto right needle.

Bind off all 12 sts **loosely** in **purl.**

FINISHING

Sew top edge of each Ear Flap to inside edge of Cap Row 7 (top of Garter Stitch), beginning 2" (5 cm) from seam.

Weave in yarn ends *(page 21).*

With Green, make two 12" (30.5 cm) 🎥 Twisted Cords *(page 21)*; sew one to bottom of each Ear Flap for tie.

🎥 Make a Green pom-pom *(Figs. 31a-c, page 21)*; sew to top of Cap.

Booties
SIDES AND BOTTOM

With Green, cast on 44 sts.

Row 1: K 17, P1, K8, P1, K 17.

Row 2 (Right side)**:** Knit across.

Rows 3-23: Repeat Rows 1 and 2, 10 times; then repeat Row 1 once **more.**

Row 24 (Eyelet row)**:** ★ K1, K2 tog, YO; repeat from ★ 2 times **more,** K 26, (YO, K2 tog, K1) 3 times.

Row 25: K 17, P1, K8, P1, K 17.

Row 26: Bind off 10 sts, K 23, bind off remaining 10 sts; cut Green: 24 sts.

TOE

With Variegated and beginning with a **purl** row, work in Stockinette Stitch until Toe measures approximately 1¼" (3 cm), ending by working a **purl** row.

SHAPING

Row 1: K2 tog across: 12 sts.

Row 2: Purl across.

Row 3: K2 tog across; cut yarn leaving a long end for sewing: 6 sts.

Finishing

🎥 Thread a yarn needle with the end and separately slip each stitch from the knitting needle onto the yarn; gather the stitches **tightly** to close, then secure end.

🎥 Weave Toe seam *(Fig. 30, page 20).*

Weave back seam from the top to the Stockinette Stitch lines; secure; do **not** cut yarn. Weave the same yarn through each of the remaining 8 sts; gather tightly and secure.

Weave in yarn ends *(page 21).*

With Green, make a 20" (51 cm) 🎥 Twisted Cord *(page 21)*. Lace Cord through Eyelet row and tie in a bow.

Designs by Beth MacDonald.

Mittens

While making these mittens (shown on page 33), you'll learn new techniques as you add on stitches for the thumb and work with stitch holders. It's a small project, so you'll learn a lot in a short time. Complete the ribbing for a small size in 30 minutes or less. Striped and multicolor variations are included to help you fashion unique mittens for yourself and everyone you know.

◖◗◗◗▭ **BEGINNER +**

SHOPPING LIST

Yarn (Medium Weight) 🄴
[3.5 ounces, 210 yards
(100 grams, 192 meters) per skein]:
☐ {65-65-80}{100-115-135}
{145-165-180} yards/
{59.5-59.5-73}{91-105-123}
{133-151-165} meters

Note: Yarn amounts are given for the **total** amount needed for a pair of mittens. When making any of the variations, divide this amount between the colors used accordingly.

Knitting Needles
Straight needles,
☐ Size 5 (3.75 mm) **and**
☐ Size 7 (4.5 mm)
or sizes needed for gauge

Additional Supplies
☐ Stitch holder - 2
☐ Marker - 2
☐ Yarn needle

SIZE INFORMATION
Selecting Correct Size Mitten:
Size indicates the number of inches (centimeters) around the palm, measured just above the thumb.

Size Note: We have printed the sizes in colors to make it easier for you to find:
- Size 5" (12.5 cm) in Blue
- Size 5½" (14 cm) in Pink
- Size 6" (15 cm) in Green
- Size 6½" (16.5 cm) in Purple
- Size 7" (18 cm) in Olive
- Size 7½" (19 cm) in Navy
- Size 8" (20.5 cm) in Brown
- Size 8½" (21.5 cm) in Red
- Size 9" (23 cm) in Yellow

Instructions in Black apply to all sizes.

GAUGE INFORMATION
See Gauge (page 13).
With larger size needles,
in Stockinette Stitch
(knit one row, purl one row),
20 sts and 28 rows = 4" (10 cm)

TECHNIQUES USED
- Using markers *(Fig. 15, page 14)*
- Knit Increase *(Figs. 17a & b, page 16)*
- Adding new stitches *(Figs. 20a & b, page 17)*
- K2 tog **(Knit 2 together,** *Fig. 21, page 18)*
- Slip 1, K1, PSSO **(Slip 1, knit 1, pass slipped stitch over,** *Fig. 24, page 19)*
- Picking up stitches *(Figs. 29a & b, page 20)*

If you come to an abbreviation, symbol, term, or punctuation that you haven't learned yet, refer to Understanding Instructions, page 12.

See To Change Colors, page 24.

INSTRUCTIONS
Ribbing
With smaller size needles, cast on {23-25-27}{29-31-33}{35-37-39} sts **loosely.**

Row 1: P1, (K1, P1) across.

Row 2 (Right side)**:** K1, (P1, K1) across.

Repeat Rows 1 and 2 until Ribbing measures approximately {2-2½-2½}{2¾-3-3}{3¼-3¼-3½}"/{5-6.5-6.5}{7-7.5-7.5}{8.5-8.5-9} cm from cast on edge, ending by working Row 1.

Body

Change to larger size needles.

Row 1: Knit across increasing {5-5-5}{5-7-7}{7-9-9} sts evenly spaced *(see Increasing Evenly Across, page 16)*: {28-30-32}{34-38-40}{42-46-48} sts.

Row 2: Purl across.

Sizes 8, 8½, and 9 Only - Rows 3 and 4: Work across in Stockinette Stitch.

SHAPING (All Sizes)

Row 1: Knit {13-14-15}{16-18-19}{20-22-23} sts, place marker, increase twice, place marker, knit across: {30-32-34}{36-40-42}{44-48-50} sts.

Row 2: Purl across.

Row 3 (Increase row)**:** Knit across to next marker, increase, knit to within one st of next marker, increase, knit across: {32-34-36}{38-42-44}{46-50-52} sts.

Repeat Rows 2 and 3, {1-2-2}{3-3-4}{4-5-5} time(s): {34-38-40}{44-48-52}{54-60-62} sts.

Work even in Stockinette Stitch until Mitten measures approximately {3¼-4-4}{4¾-5-5¼}{5¾-6-6¼}" /{8.5-10-10}{12-12.5-13.5}{14.5-15-16} cm from cast on edge, ending by working a **purl** row.

THUMB

Row 1: Knit across to next marker and slip these {13-14-15}{16-18-19}{20-22-23} sts just worked onto st holder, remove marker, add on one st; knit added on st, knit across to next marker, remove marker, **turn**; add on one st, slip remaining sts onto second st holder: {10-12-12}{14-14-16}{16-18-18} sts.

Work even until Thumb measures approximately {1¼-1½-1¾}{2-2¼-2½}{2½-2¾-2¾}"/{3-4-4.5}{5-5.5-6.5}{6.5-7-7} cm, ending by working a **purl** row.

Next Row: K2 tog across: {5-6-6}{7-7-8}{8-9-9} sts.

Cut yarn leaving a long end.

Thread a yarn needle with the end and separately slip each stitch from the knitting needle onto the yarn; gather the stitches **tightly** to close, then secure end.

Weave seam *(Fig. 30, page 20)*.

HAND

With **right** side facing, slip sts from first st holder onto needle; with same needle, pick up a st in each of 2 added on sts at base of Thumb; slip sts from second st holder onto empty needle and knit across: {28-30-32}{34-38-40}{42-46-48} sts.

Work even until piece measures approximately {4¾-6-6}{7-7½-7¾}{8½-8¾-9¼}" /{12-15-15}{18-19-19.5}{21.5-22-23.5} cm from cast on edge, ending by working a **knit** row.

Next Row: Purl {14-15-16}{17-19-20}{21-23-24} sts, place marker, purl across.

SHAPING

Row 1: K2, slip 1 as if to **knit**, K1, PSSO, knit across to within 3 sts of next marker, K2 tog, K1, slip marker, K1, slip 1 as if to **knit**, K1, PSSO, knit across to last 4 sts, K2 tog, K2: {24-26-28}{30-34-36}{38-42-44} sts.

Row 2: Purl across.

Repeat Rows 1 and 2, {1-2-3}{3-4-5}{5-5-5} time(s): {20-18-16}{18-18-16}{18-22-24} sts.

Next Row: K2 tog across: {10-9-8}{9-9-8}{9-11-12} sts.

Cut yarn leaving a long end.

Thread a yarn needle with the end and separately slip each stitch from the knitting needle onto the yarn; gather the stitches tightly to close, then secure end. Weave seam.

Weave in yarn ends *(page 21)*.

VARIATIONS

3-COLOR STRIPES

Work Ribbing in Main Color (Pink). Complete Mitten working in the following color sequence: 1 Row **each** of Color A (Green), Color B (Orange), and Main Color (Pink), carrying the yarns loosely along the edge and working the Thumb with Main Color.

MULTI-COLORS

Work Ribbing in Color A (Green), Body in Color B (Pink), Thumb in Color C (Orange), and Hand in Color D (Purple). Work second Mitten, same as the first, switching the positions of the colors, or with completely different colors.

Designs by Mary Lamb Becker.

Pillow

This classic cable Pillow is made with a lacy "yarn over" design. As impressive as cables are, you'll soon see that they aren't hard to make. Practice making a few cables by working the Gauge Swatch. Soon you'll be able to complete several rows of the Pillow in 10 minutes! What a lovely way to decorate a room and show off your new skill at the same time!

BEGINNER +

Finished Size: 14" (35.5) square

SHOPPING LIST

Yarn (Medium Weight)

[7 ounces, 364 yards
(198 grams, 333 meters) per skein]:

☐ 2 skeins

Knitting Needles

Straight needles,

☐ Size 8 (5 mm)

   or size needed for gauge

Additional Supplies

☐ Cable needle (see note below)

☐ Yarn needle

☐ 14" (35.5 cm) Square pillow form

Note: Cable needles have a point on each end and are available in several shapes and sizes. The size of the cable needle does not have to be the same size as the needles with which you are knitting, but it should not be bigger or it will stretch the stitches out of shape.

GAUGE INFORMATION

See Gauge (page 13).

In pattern,

   3 repeats (24 sts) = 4½" (11.5 cm);

   24 rows = 4" (10 cm)

Gauge Swatch: 4¾"w x 4"h
   (12 cm x 10 cm)

Cast on 26 sts **loosely**.

Work same as Pillow Cover for 24 rows.

Bind off **loosely** in pattern.

TECHNIQUES USED

- YO (Yarn overs, *Fig. 19a, page 17*)
- K2 tog (**Knit 2 together,** *Fig. 21, page 18*)
- Slip 1, K1, PSSO
  (**Slip 1, knit 1, pass slipped stitch over,** *Fig. 24, page 19*)

—— STITCH GUIDE ——

CABLE (uses next 6 sts)

Slip next 3 sts onto cable needle as if to **purl** and hold them in **back** of work, K3 from left needle (*Fig. 32a*), K3 from cable needle being sure that the first st you knit is the first one you slipped onto the cable needle (*Fig. 32b*).

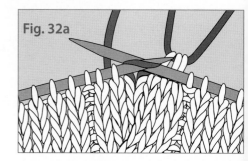

Fig. 32a

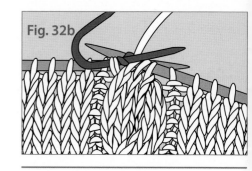

Fig. 32b

If you come to an abbreviation, symbol, term, or punctuation that you haven't learned yet, refer to Understanding Instructions, page 12.

INSTRUCTIONS
Pillow Cover (Make 2)
Cast on 74 sts **loosely**.

Row 1 AND ALL WRONG SIDE ROWS: K2, (P6, K2) across.

Row 2 (Right side)**:** P2, (K6, P2) across.

Row 4: P2, (work Cable, P2) across.

Row 6: P2, (K6, P2) across.

Row 8: P2, ★ K1, YO, K2 tog, K3, P2; repeat from ★ across.

Row 10: P2, ★ slip 1 as if to **knit**, K1, PSSO, YO, K4, P2; repeat from ★ across.

Row 12: P2, ★ K1, YO, K2 tog, K3, P2; repeat from ★ across.

Row 14: P2, (K6, P2) across.

Row 16: P2, (work Cable, P2) across.

Row 18: P2, (K6, P2) across.

Row 20: P2, ★ K3, slip 1 as if to **knit**, K1, PSSO, YO, K1, P2; repeat from ★ across.

Row 22: P2, ★ K4, YO, K2 tog, P2; repeat from ★ across.

Row 24: P2, ★ K3, slip 1 as if to **knit**, K1, PSSO, YO, K1, P2; repeat from ★ across.

Repeat Rows 1-24 for pattern until Pillow measures approximately 13" (33 cm) from cast on edge, ending by working a **wrong** side row.

Bind off all sts **loosely** maintaining knit and purl pattern (do **not** work cables, decreases, or yarn overs).

Cover pillow form with fabric, if desired.

With **wrong** sides together, matching stitches and rows, sew around three sides, insert pillow form and sew last side.

Weave in yarn ends (page 21).

Baby Blanket

This precious Baby Blanket is knit with soft yarn on a circular needle in the same way you've been knitting on straight needles, allowing you to work with more stitches at a time. Before long you'll find yourself able to knit a few rows in just 20 minutes. You'll enjoy seeing a precious baby wrapped in this sweet eyelet pattern that shows off your new hobby.

◖◻◻◻◻ **BEGINNER +**

Finished Size: 34" x 46" (86.5 cm x 117 cm)

GAUGE INFORMATION

See Gauge (page 13).

In pattern,
16 sts and 26 rows = 4" (10 cm)

TECHNIQUES USED

🎥 YO (**Yarn overs,** *Fig. 19a,*
page 17)

🎥 SSK (**Slip, slip, knit,** *Figs. 23a-c,*
page 18)

🎥 Slip 1, K2 tog, PSSO
(**Slip 1, Knit 2 together, pass
slipped stitch over,**
Fig. 25, page 19)

If you come to an abbreviation, symbol, term, or punctuation that you haven't learned yet, refer to Understanding Instructions, page 12.

INSTRUCTIONS

Cast on 137 sts.

Rows 1-8: Knit across.

Row 9: K5, purl across to last 5 sts, K5.

Row 10: Knit across.

Row 11: K5, purl across to last 5 sts, K5.

Row 12: K7, YO, slip 1 as if to **knit**, K2 tog, PSSO, ★ YO, K5, YO, slip 1 as if to **knit**, K2 tog, PSSO; repeat from ★ across to last 7 sts, YO, K7.

Row 13: K5, purl across to last 5 sts, K5.

Row 14: K8, YO, SSK, (K6, YO, SSK) across to last 7 sts, K7.

Row 15: K5, purl across to last 5 sts, K5.

Row 16: Knit across.

Row 17: K5, purl across to last 5 sts, K5.

Row 18: K 11, YO, slip 1 as if to **knit**, K2 tog, PSSO, ★ YO, K5, YO, slip 1 as if to **knit**, K2 tog, PSSO; repeat from ★ across to last 11 sts, YO, K 11.

Row 19: K5, purl across to last 5 sts, K5.

Row 20: K 12, YO, SSK, (K6, YO, SSK) across to last 11 sts, K 11.

Repeat Rows 9-20 for pattern until Blanket measures approximately 45" (114.5 cm) from cast on edge, ending by working Row 17.

Last 8 rows: Knit across.

Bind off all sts in **knit**.

Weave in yarn ends *(page 21)*.

Dog Coat

The Dog Coat is made using a double Seed Stitch pattern, increases, and decreases. The pattern is not complicated, but the neck shaping is new, so take your time and read each instruction carefully. In just 10 minutes, you'll be able to knit several rows! On your next walk, you can really show off your new talent as your favorite pooch wears the colorful coat in style!

⬛◻◻◻ **BEGINNER +**

SHOPPING LIST

Yarn (Medium Weight)

[7 ounces, 364 yards (198 grams, 333 meters) per skein]:

☐ 1 skein

Knitting Needles

Straight needles,

☐ Size 7 (4.5 mm)

or size needed for gauge

Additional Supplies

☐ Stitch holder

☐ Markers - 2

☐ ¾" (19 mm) Buttons - 2

☐ Yarn needle

SIZE INFORMATION

Finished Measurement:

(from neck to base of tail)

Small: 12" (30.5 cm)

Medium: 14" (35.5 cm)

Large: 16" (40.5 cm)

X-Large: 18" (45.5 cm)

Size Note: We have printed the sizes in colors to make it easier for you to find:

- Size Small in Blue
- Size Medium in Pink
- Size Large in Green
- Size X-Large in Red

Instructions in Black apply to all sizes.

GAUGE INFORMATION

When making a garment, correct gauge is critical to ensure fit. *See Gauge (page 13).*

In pattern,

20 sts and 26 rows = 4" (10 cm)

If you come to an abbreviation, symbol, term, or punctuation that you haven't learned yet, refer to Understanding Instructions, page 12.

TECHNIQUES USED

🎥 Using markers (*Fig. 15, page 14*)

🎥 Knit Increase (*Figs. 17a & b, page 16*)

🎥 YO (**Yarn overs,** *Fig. 19a, page 17*)

🎥 K2 tog (**Knit 2 together,** *Fig. 21, page 18*)

🎥 Slip 1, K1, PSSO (**Slip 1, knit 1, pass slipped stitch over,** *Fig. 24, page 19*)

🎥 Picking up sts (*Fig. 29b, page 20*)

INSTRUCTIONS
Body

Cast on 40{44-52-56} sts.

Row 1: Knit across.

Rows 2-7: K1, increase, knit across to last 2 sts, increase, K1: 52{56-64-68} sts.

Row 8 (Right side)**:** K6, place marker, knit across to last 6 sts, place marker, K6.

Note: Loop a short piece of yarn around any stitch to mark Row 8 as **right** side.

Rows 9 and 10: Knit across to first marker, (P2, K2) across to next marker, knit across.

Rows 11 and 12: Knit across to first marker, (K2, P2) across to next marker, knit across.

Repeat Rows 9-12 for pattern until Body measures approximately 11{13-15-17}"/28{33-38-43} cm from cast on edge, ending by working a **wrong** side row.

NECK SHAPING

Both sides of the Neck are worked at the same time, using separate yarn for each side. This guarantees that both sides will be the same length. **Maintain established pattern throughout.**

To maintain established pattern, simply look at a stitch as it faces you and determine whether it is a knit or purl stitch, then proceed with the proper stitch to continue the pattern. *(See Basic Fabrics, page 9.)*

Row 1: Work across 18{18-20-22} sts, slip next 16{20-24-24} sts onto st holder; with second yarn, work across: 18{18-20-22} sts **each** side.

Row 2 (Decrease row)**:** Work across to within 2 sts of Neck edge, K2 tog; with second yarn, slip 1 as if to **knit**, K1, PSSO, work across: 17{17-19-21} sts **each** side.

Rows 3 and 4: Repeat Row 2: 15{15-17-19} sts **each** side.

Continue to decrease one stitch at **each** Neck edge, every other row, 3{3-4-5} times: 12{12-13-14} sts **each** side.

Work even until Coat measures approximately 14{16½-18½-21}"/35.5{42-47-53.5} cm from cast on edge, ending by working a **wrong** side row.

Bind off all sts.

Finishing
NECKBAND

With **right** side facing, pick up 18{22-22-24} sts along right Neck edge, slip 16{20-24-24} sts from st holder onto empty needle and knit across, pick up 18{22-22-24} sts along left Neck edge: 52{64-68-72} sts.

Knit 8 rows.

Bind off all sts in **knit**.

BAND

With **right** side facing and beginning 5½{6½-7½-8½}"/14{16.5-19-21.5} cm down from left bound off edge, pick up 10 sts evenly spaced across 2" (5 cm).

Knit every row until Coat fits snugly around Dog's chest.

Next Row (Buttonhole row)**:** K2, YO (buttonhole), K2 tog, K2, K2 tog, YO (buttonhole), K2.

Knit 3 rows.

Bind off all sts in **knit**.

Sew end of Right Neck to end of Left Neck.

Weave in yarn ends.

Sew Buttons to Body, opposite Band.

Design by Evie Rosen.

Textured Stripes Afghan

The Textured Stripes Afghan (shown on page 43) is a great example of the creative possibilities of your newly learned skills. This cozy design is knitted while holding two strands of yarn together as if they were one strand, so you get a beautiful blanket in a hurry. Also, some of the rows are worked while carrying two colors of yarn across (for a total of four strands) and bringing three stitches of one color to the front repeatedly to create a dimensional effect. With a little practice, you'll be able to complete a stripe in about 30 minutes! Imagine your satisfaction when you curl up under this attractive afghan that you made all by yourself!

●▢▢▢ **BEGINNER +**

Finished Size: 46" x 60" (117 cm x 152.5 cm)

SHOPPING LIST

Yarn (Medium Weight)
[5 ounces, 256 yards
(141 grams, 234 meters) per skein]:

☐ Dk Teal - 6 skeins

☐ Lt Teal - 5 skeins

☐ Green - 3 skeins

Knitting Needle

29" (73.5 cm) Circular needle,

☐ Size 8 (5 mm)

or size needed for gauge

Additional Supplies

☐ Yarn needle

GAUGE INFORMATION

See Gauge (page 13).

With two strands of yarn held
together, in Garter Stitch
(knit every row), 9 sts = 4" (10 cm)

The entire Afghan is worked holding two strands together as if they were one strand and using a circular needle in the same way you've been knitting on straight needles, allowing you to work with more stitches at a time.

If you come to an abbreviation, symbol, term, or punctuation that you haven't learned yet, refer to Understanding Instructions, page 12.

See To Change Colors, page 24.

TECHNIQUES USED

■ Slip 1 as if to purl (*Fig. 14a, page 14*)

■ tbl (**Through back loop,** *Figs. 12 and 13, page 14*)

■ K3 tog (**Knit 3 together,** *Fig. 22, page 18*)

INSTRUCTIONS

With Dk Teal, cast on 103 sts.

Rows 1-6: Knit across; at end of Row 6, cut Dk Teal.

Rows 7 and 8: With Green, knit across; at end of Row 8, cut Green.

Rows 9-11: With Lt Teal, knit across.

Row 12: Purl across; do **not** cut Lt Teal.

Row 13: 📹 With yarn in **back** slip 1 as if to **purl**, ★ with Dk Teal, (K, K tbl, K) **all** in next st, with yarn in **back** slip 1 as if to **purl**; repeat from ★ across: 205 sts.

Row 14: With yarn in **back** slip 1 as if to **purl**, ★ K3 tog, with yarn in **front** slip 1 as if to **purl**; repeat from ★ across, cut Dk Teal: 103 sts.

Row 15: With Lt Teal, knit across.

Row 16: Purl across.

Rows 17 and 18: Knit across; at end of Row 18, cut Lt Teal.

Rows 19 and 20: With Green, knit across; at end of Row 20, cut Green

Rows 21-23: With Dk Teal, knit across.

Row 24: Purl across; do **not** cut Dk Teal.

Row 25: With yarn in **back** slip 1 as if to **purl**, ★ with Lt Teal, (K, K tbl, K) **all** in next st, with yarn in **back** slip 1 as if to **purl**; repeat from ★ across: 205 sts.

Row 26: With yarn in **back** slip 1 as if to **purl**, ★ K3 tog, with yarn in **front** slip 1 as if to **purl**; repeat from ★ across, cut Lt Teal: 103 sts.

Row 27: With Dk Teal, knit across.

Row 28: Purl across.

Rows 29 and 30: Knit across; at end of Row 30, cut Dk Teal.

Repeat Rows 7-30 for pattern until afghan measures approximately 58½" (148.5 cm) from cast on edge; ending by working Row 20; cut Green.

Last 6 Rows: With Dk Teal, knit across.

Bind all sts in **knit**.

Design by Melissa Leapman.

Vest

A vest is a great way to learn how to knit a garment. Stitches for the armhole and Front Bands are added on and worked as you knit the Body, eliminating extra finishing steps. You can have the Ribbing knit in as little as 20 minutes and be on your way to completing your first garment. You'll enjoy getting compliments on your new skills when you wear this appealing vest.

◼️◻️◻️◻️ **BEGINNER +**

SHOPPING LIST

Yarn (Medium Weight) 🄌

[3.5 ounces, 210 yards
(100 grams, 192 meters) per skein]:

☐ 3{3-4} skeins

Knitting Needles

Straight needles,

☐ Size 9 (5.5 mm)

or size needed for gauge

Additional Supplies

☐ Stitch holders - 2

☐ Yarn needle

SIZE INFORMATION

Finished Chest Measurement:

Small - 36" (91.5 cm)

Medium - 40" (101.5 cm)

Large - 44" (112 cm)

Size Note: We have printed the sizes in colors to make it easier for you to find:

- Size Small in Blue
- Size Medium in Pink
- Size Large in Green

Instructions in Black apply to all sizes.

GAUGE INFORMATION

When making a garment, correct gauge is critical to ensure fit. *See Gauge (page 13).*

In Stockinette Stitch

(knit one row, purl one row),
16 sts and 22 rows = 4" (10 cm)

If you come to an abbreviation, symbol, term, or punctuation that you haven't learned yet, refer to Understanding Instructions, page 12.

TECHNIQUES USED

- 🎥 Knit Increase *(Figs. 17a & b, page 16)*
- 🎥 Adding new stitches *(Figs. 20a & b, page 17)*
- 🎥 K2 tog **(Knit 2 together,** *Fig. 21, page 18)*
- 🎥 SSK **(Slip, slip, knit,** *Figs. 23a-c, page 18)*
- 🎥 P2 tog **(Purl 2 together,** *Fig. 26, page 19)*
- 🎥 SSP **(Slip, slip, purl,** *Fig. 28, page 19)*

INSTRUCTIONS
Back
RIBBING

Cast on 74{82-90} sts **loosely**.

Work in K1, P1 ribbing for 3 rows increasing one stitch at end of last row: 75{83-91} sts.

BODY

Work in Stockinette Stitch until Back measures approximately 11½{12-12½}"/29{30.5-32} cm from cast on edge, ending by working a **purl** row.

ARMHOLE SHAPING

Row 1: Add on 3 sts (Armhole band), K3 (same sts added on), SSK, knit across to last 2 sts, K2 tog, **turn**; add on 3 sts (Armhole band): 79{87-95} sts.

Row 2 (Decrease row): K3, P2 tog, purl across to last 5 sts, SSP, K3: 77{85-93} sts.

Row 3 (Decrease row): K3, SSK, knit across to last 5 sts, K2 tog, K3: 75{83-91} sts.

Rows 4 thru 7{9-11}: Repeat Rows 2 and 3, 2{3-4} times: 67{71-75} sts.

Row 8{10-12}: K3, purl across to last 3 sts, K3.

Row 9{11-13} (Decrease row): K3, SSK, knit across to last 5 sts, K2 tog, K3: 65{69-73} sts.

Rows 10{12-14} and 11{13-15}: Repeat Rows 8{10-12} and 9{11-13}: 63{67-71} sts.

Row 12{14-16}: K3, purl across to last 3 sts, K3.

Row 13{15-17}: Knit across.

Row 14{16-18}: K3, purl across to last 3 sts, K3.

Row 15{17-19} (Decrease row): K3, SSK, knit across to last 5 sts, K2 tog, K3: 61{65-69} sts.

Rows 16{18-20} thru 19{21-23}: Repeat Rows 12{14-16} thru 15{17-19}: 59{63-67} sts.

Repeat Rows 12{14-16} and 13{15-17} until Armholes measure approximately 7½{8-8½}" /19{20.5-21.5} cm, ending by working a **wrong** side row.

SHOULDER SHAPING

To shape the shoulders, bind off stitches in pattern at the beginning of each row as indicated.

Row 1: Bind off 5{6-6} sts at the beginning of the row, knit across: 54{57-61} sts.

Row 2: Bind off 5{6-6} sts at the beginning of the row, purl across: 49{51-55} sts.

Rows 3 and 4: Bind off 6 sts at the beginning of the row, work across: 37{39-43} sts.

Rows 5 and 6: Bind off 6{6-7} sts at the beginning of the row, work across: 25{27-29} sts.

Slip remaining sts onto st holder; cut yarn.

Front

Work same as Back through Row 8{10-12} of Armhole Shaping: 67{71-75} sts.

NECK & ARMHOLE SHAPING

Both sides of the Neck are worked at the same time, using separate yarn for each side. This guarantees that both sides will be the same length. The semicolon (;) separates the instructions for each side and is the signal for you to drop your first yarn and begin working with the second yarn.

Row 1 (Decrease row): K3, SSK, K 25{27-29}, K2 tog, **turn**, add on 3 sts **loosely** (Front Band), **turn**; with second yarn, K3 (Front Band), SSK, knit across to last 5 sts, K2 tog, K3: 33{35-37} sts **each** side.

Row 2: K3, purl across to within 3 sts of Neck edge, K3; with second yarn, K3, purl across to last 3 sts, K3.

Row 3 (Decrease row): K3, SSK, knit across to within 5 sts of Neck edge, K2 tog, K3; with second yarn, K3, SSK, knit across to last 5 sts, K2 tog, K3: 31{33-35} sts **each** side.

Row 4: K3, purl across to within 3 sts of Neck edge, K3; with second yarn, K3, purl across to last 3 sts, K3.

Row 5 (Decrease row): Knit across to within 5 sts of Neck edge, K2 tog, K3; with second yarn, K3, SSK, knit across: 30{32-34} sts **each** side.

Rows 6-11: Repeat Rows 2-5 once, then repeat Rows 2 and 3 once **more**: 25{27-29} sts **each** side.

FOR SIZES MEDIUM & LARGE ONLY
Rows 12 thru {15-19}: Repeat Rows 4 and 5, {2-4} times: 25 sts **each** side.

FOR ALL SIZES
Row 12{16-20}: K3, purl across to within 3 sts of Neck edge, K3; with second yarn, K3, purl across to last 3 sts, K3.

Row 13{17-21}: Knit across; with second yarn, knit across.

Row 14{18-22}: K3, purl across to within 3 sts of Neck edge, K3; with second yarn, K3, purl across to last 3 sts, K3.

Row 15{19-23} (Decrease row)**:** Knit across to within 5 sts of Neck edge, K2 tog, K3; with second yarn, K3, SSK, knit across: 24 sts **each** side.

Rows 16{20-24} thru 31: Repeat Rows 12{16-20} thru 15{19-23}, 4{3-2} times: 20{21-22} sts **each** side.

Repeat Rows 12{16-20} and 13{17-21} until Armholes measure same as Back to Shoulder Shaping, ending by working a **wrong** side row.

SHOULDER SHAPING

Row 1: Bind off 5{6-6} sts at Armhole edge, knit across; with second yarn, knit across.

Row 2: Bind off 5{6-6} sts at Armhole edge, purl across to within 3 sts of Neck edge, K3; with second yarn, K3, purl across: 15{15-16} sts **each** side.

Row 3: Bind off 6 sts at Armhole edge, knit across; with second yarn, knit across.

Row 4: Bind off 6 sts at Armhole edge, purl across to within 3 sts of Neck edge, K3; with second yarn, K3, purl across: 9{9-10} sts **each** side.

Row 5: Bind off 9{9-10} sts; with second yarn, knit across.

Row 6: Bind off 6{6-7} sts, K2: 3 sts.

Slip remaining sts onto st holder; cut yarn.

Finishing

Sew shoulder seams, leaving 3 sts at each Neck edge free (Front Band).

BACK NECK BAND

Rather than making the Back Neck Band separately and then sewing it to the Back, you will work in 🎥 short rows, which are rows that are not worked all the way from one end to the other. Each right side row works across 2 stitches from the Front Band, then a decrease is made using the last stitch on the Front Band and the next stitch on the Back neck. Leaving the remaining stitches unworked, you will stop, **turn** the work, and work the next row in the opposite direction.

Begin working in short rows as follows: Slip 25{27-29} sts from Back st holder onto needle; slip 3 sts from Right Front st holder onto same needle.

Row 1: K2, K2 tog, leave remaining sts unworked.

Row 2: Turn; knit across.

Repeat Rows 1 and 2 until only 3 sts remain, ending by working Row 2.

Bind off remaining 3 sts.

Sew Back Neck Band and Left Front Band together.

Sew bottom of Left Front Band to **wrong** side behind Right Front Band.

🎥 Weave side seams (*Fig. 30, page 20*).

Yarn Information

Projects in this book were made using Medium Weight Yarn. Any brand of the specified weight of yarn may be used. It is best to refer to the yardage/meters when determining how many balls or skeins to purchase. Remember, to arrive at the finished size, it is the GAUGE/TENSION that is important, not the brand of yarn. For your convenience, listed below are the specific yarns used to create our photography models.

DISHCLOTHS
Lily® Sugar'n Cream®
Blue - #0026 Light Blue
Variegated - #203 Blue Shadow

SCARF & HAT
Red Heart® Super Saver®
Grey - #0400 Grey Heather
Burgundy - #0376 Burgundy
Lt Grey - #0341 Lt Grey

BABY GIFT SET
Red Heart® Soft Baby Steps®
Variegated - #9939 Tickle
Green - #9630 Lime

MITTENS
Patons® Classic Wool Worsted™
One Color
Variegated - #77014 Forest
3-Colored Stripes
Rose - #77404 Orchid
Green - #00240 Leaf Green
Orange - #77605 Pumpkin
Multi-Colored
Green - #00240 Leaf Green
Orange - #77605 Pumpkin
Rose - #77404 Orchid
Purple - #00212 Royal Purple

PILLOW
Red Heart® Super Saver®
#0313 Aran

BABY BLANKET
Caron® Simply Soft®
#9719 Soft Pink

DOG COAT
Red Heart® Super Saver®
#0319 Cherry Red

TEXTURED STRIPES AFGHAN
Red Heart® Soft®
Dk Teal - #9518 Teal
Lt Teal - #9520 Seafoam
Green - #9623 Spearmint

VEST
Patons® Classic Wool Worsted™
#77531 Currant